HIP-HOP

Alicia Keys
Ashanti
Beyoncé
Black Eyed Peas
Busta Rhymes
Chris Brown
Christina Aguilera
Ciara
Cypress Hill
Daddy Yankee
DMX
Don Omar
Dr. Dre
Eminem
Fat Joe
50 Cent
The Game
Hip-Hop: A Short History
Hip-Hop Around the World
Ice Cube
Ivy Queen
Jay-Z
Jennifer Lopez
Juelz Santana
Kanye West

Lil Wayne
LL Cool J
Lloyd Banks
Ludacris
Mariah Carey
Mary J. Blige
Missy Elliot
Nas
Nelly
Notorious B.I.G.
OutKast
Pharrell Williams
Pitbull
Queen Latifah
Reverend Run (of Run DMC)
Sean "Diddy" Combs
Snoop Dogg
T.I.
Tupac
Usher
Will Smith
Wu-Tang Clan
Xzibit
Young Jeezy
Yung Joc

Jennifer Lopez is a phenomenon. Not only is she a well-known actress and fashion star, she's a music superstar. Not bad for "Jenny from the block."

Hip-Hop

Jennifer Lopez

MaryJo Lemmens

Mason Crest Publishers

Jennifer Lopez

Produced by Harding House Publishing Service, Inc.
201 Harding Avenue, Vestal, NY 13850.

MASON CREST PUBLISHERS INC.
370 Reed Road
Broomall, Pennsylvania 19008
(866)MCP-BOOK (toll free)
www.masoncrest.com

Printed in the United States of America

First Printing

9 8 7 6 5 4 3 2 1

Library of Congress Cataloging-in-Publication Data

Lemmens, MaryJo.
  Jennifer Lopez / MaryJo Lemmens.
     p. cm. — (Hip-hop)
  Includes index.
  ISBN-13: 978-1-4222-0296-8
  ISBN: 978-1-4222-0077-3 (series)
  1. Lopez, Jennifer, 1970—Juvenile literature. 2. Actors—United States—Biography—Juvenile literature. 3. Singers—United States—Biography—Juvenile literature. I. Title.
  PN2287.L634L46 2008
  791.43'028'092—dc22

                                    2007028136

Publisher's notes:
• All quotations in this book come from original sources and contain the spelling and grammatical inconsistencies of the original text.

• The Web sites mentioned in this book were active at the time of publication. The publisher is not responsible for Web sites that have changed their addresses or discontinued operation since the date of publication. The publisher will review and update the Web site addresses each time the book is reprinted.

DISCLAIMER: The following story has been thoroughly researched, and to the best of our knowledge, represents a true story. While every possible effort has been made to ensure accuracy, the publisher will not assume liability for damages caused by inaccuracies in the data, and makes no warranty on the accuracy of the information contained herein. This story has not been authorized nor endorsed by Jennifer Lopez.

Contents

Hip-Hop Time Line   6

1 A Shining Star   9

2 The Girl from Castle Hill   15

3 Out on Her Own   25

4 Jenny From the Block   35

5 Finding Herself Again   45

Chronology   52

Accomplishments and Awards   54

Further Reading/Internet Resources   59

Glossary   61

Index   63

About the Author   64

Picture Credits   64

Hip-Hop Time Line

1976 Grandmaster Flash and the Furious Five emerge as one of the first battlers and freestylers.

1984 The track "Roxanne Roxanne" sparks the first diss war.

1970s DJ Kool Herc pioneers the use of breaks, isolations, and repeats using two turntables.

1988 Hip-hop record sales reach 100 million annually.

1982 Afrika Bambaataa tours Europe in another hip-hop first.

1970s Grafitti artist Vic begins tagging on New York subways.

1980 Rapper Kurtis Blow sells a million records and makes the first nationwide TV appearance for a hip-hop artist.

1985 The film *Krush Groove*, about the rise of Def Jam Records, is released.

1970   1980

1970s The central elements of the hip-hop culture begin to emerge in the Bronx, New York City.

1983 Ice-T releases his first singles, marking the earliest examples of gangsta rap.

1986 Run DMC cover Aerosmith's "Walk this Way" and appear on the cover of *Rolling Stone*.

1979 "Rapper's Delight," by The Sugarhill Gang, goes gold.

1974 Afrika Bambaataa organizes the Universal Zulu Nation.

1984 *Graffitti Rock*, the first hip-hop television program, premieres.

1988 MTV premieres *Yo! MTV Raps*.

1981 Grandmaster Flash and the Furious Five release *Adventures on the Wheels of Steel*.

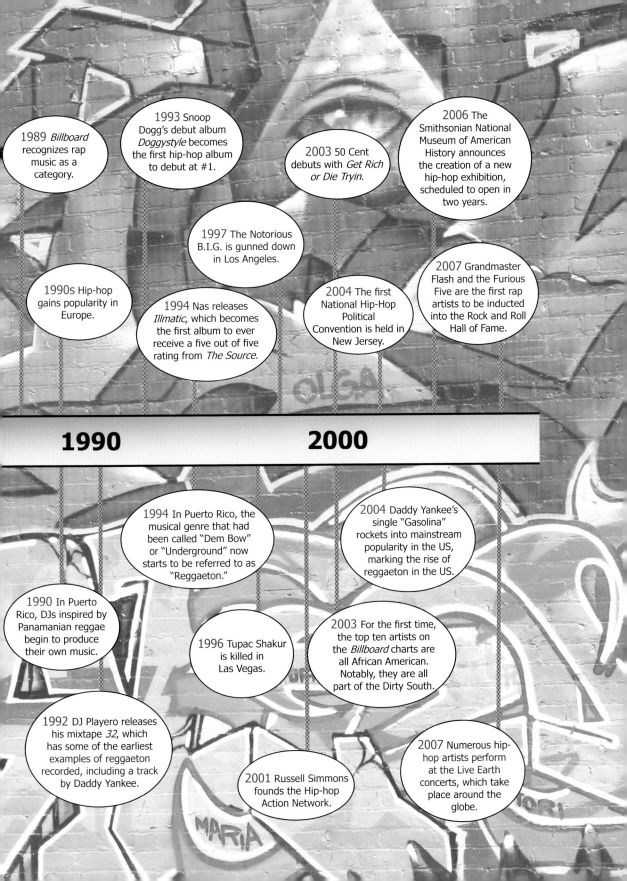

1989 *Billboard* recognizes rap music as a category.

1993 Snoop Dogg's debut album *Doggystyle* becomes the first hip-hop album to debut at #1.

2003 50 Cent debuts with *Get Rich or Die Tryin*.

2006 The Smithsonian National Museum of American History announces the creation of a new hip-hop exhibition, scheduled to open in two years.

1997 The Notorious B.I.G. is gunned down in Los Angeles.

1990s Hip-hop gains popularity in Europe.

1994 Nas releases *Illmatic*, which becomes the first album to ever receive a five out of five rating from *The Source*.

2004 The first National Hip-Hop Political Convention is held in New Jersey.

2007 Grandmaster Flash and the Furious Five are the first rap artists to be inducted into the Rock and Roll Hall of Fame.

1990

2000

1994 In Puerto Rico, the musical genre that had been called "Dem Bow" or "Underground" now starts to be referred to as "Reggaeton."

2004 Daddy Yankee's single "Gasolina" rockets into mainstream popularity in the US, marking the rise of reggaeton in the US.

1990 In Puerto Rico, DJs inspired by Panamanian reggae begin to produce their own music.

1996 Tupac Shakur is killed in Las Vegas.

2003 For the first time, the top ten artists on the *Billboard* charts are all African American. Notably, they are all part of the Dirty South.

1992 DJ Playero releases his mixtape *32*, which has some of the earliest examples of reggaeton recorded, including a track by Daddy Yankee.

2001 Russell Simmons founds the Hip-hop Action Network.

2007 Numerous hip-hop artists perform at the Live Earth concerts, which take place around the globe.

Jennifer Lopez has come a long way through hard work and talent. People all over the world respect her for what she's been able to accomplish.

A Shining Star

Music pounded, lights pulsed, and sparks exploded into the air, but everyone's eyes were fixed on the woman in the middle of the stage. In a halo of lights and smoke, Jennifer Lopez belted out "Que Hiciste," a song from her newest album. It's a passionate song about a perfect love destroyed by an imperfect lover. Most of the audience couldn't understand a single word—the song was all in Spanish—but they didn't need to. Jennifer's energy kept them all enthralled, and her passion communicated the song's emotions. As the last notes died away, the audience roared its approval with cheers and a standing ovation.

The live performance happened on one of the world's most popular shows, *American Idol*, in front of millions of viewers. Jennifer Lopez wasn't, of course, a contestant on the hit show; she was a guest **mentor**. As a mentor, the pop star coached the show's contestants, encouraging them to find the passion and emotion in every song. And when she gave her guest performance, she showed them just how to do it. For a singer who has numerous studio albums but never gone on tour, it was proof that Jennifer Lopez has the live-performance muscle to back up her star status.

The Spanish song was something new for Jennifer. Although she is of Puerto Rican heritage and has always had great support from America's Latino community, her previous albums were in English. In fact, she didn't even learn to speak fluent Spanish, her family's native language, until she was an adult. Her new Spanish-language album embraces her Latino heritage in a whole new way, but for most of her singing career, Jennifer Lopez has been a mainstream pop and **R&B** artist with a strong hip-hop influence.

Jennifer, however, is a multi-talented performer whose work defies definition. She has never limited her career to just one thing—she is a dancer, an actress, and a singer—so it shouldn't be surprising that she doesn't limit her music to just one style. She is pop, R&B, hip-hop, dance, Latin, and sometimes even a little funk and rock. Like the New York City of her birth, Jennifer is a great mix of styles and influences that blend into something new, unique, and wonderful, something that attracts people, excites them, and makes them call out for more.

Born to Perform

Jennifer Lopez's charisma has made her a star as a singer, an actor, and as a dancer. She has been drawn to the stage ever since she was a little girl. In an interview with Prairie Miller of *NY Rock*, Jennifer explained that her determination to be a performer began when she was very young:

"I just knew that was what I wanted to do. I was going to perform as a singer; I was going to perform as a dancer, and I was, you know, going to do movies and be an actress. I was going to do it or die trying. That's what my life was."

Jennifer was as determined as they come, but it was going to be a hard road to success. When Jennifer was growing up, there weren't many names that sounded like Lopez up in Hollywood's glittering lights. She was a Puerto Rican American girl growing up in an era when many Latino performers tried to hide their roots for fear of discrimination. Some earlier Latinas, like Rita Hayworth and Raquel Welch, did so by taking English-sounding stage names. Rita Hayworth's birth name was Margarita Carmen Dolorex Cansino. Raquel Welch began life as Jo Raquel Tejada. But names like that didn't sit well with some white audiences.

That, however, didn't discourage Jennifer. She knew being Latina on stage and in Hollywood would be hard. She knew people, if they hired her at all, would try to pigeonhole her, only offering her certain stereotypical roles written for Latino performers. She knew that, the way Hollywood was back then, she'd be more likely to land a bit part as a hot-blooded flamenco dancer or gang member's girlfriend than as an educated career woman or the leading lady in a romantic comedy. But Jennifer believed she could play any role, and she was determined to show everyone that she could do it all. In her interview with *NY Rock*, she explained that by being realistic and meeting people's **stereotypes** head on, she was able to take control of her career and rise to the top of Hollywood's A-list:

"I'd be stupid not to take into consideration that there are certain things people will not consider me for because my name is Lopez. And I know I can do any

kind of role. I don't want anybody to say, 'Oh, she can't pull this off.' So those are barriers you have to overcome. . . . And that's why from the beginning I made a conscious decision to make certain choices to not ever be put in one category. You know, like this is what she does. She's a Latin actress who just

Jennifer has starred in many roles since she broke into film with *Selena*. This photo of Jennifer is from the premiere of her film *Monster-in-Law*, in which she costars with screen legend Jane Fonda.

does these types of role. So I always chose things, and passed on other things because of that."

Hard Work Pays Off

Jennifer was right. From starring roles as the famous Latin singer Selena, to the love interest of a powerful senatorial candidate, a psychiatrist doing groundbreaking research, and a reporter investigating murders in a Mexican border town, she has shown the world that she can take on any type of role (not just ones made for Latina performers). She has a **mainstream** film and a popular music career, yet she has never denied her Puerto Rican heritage. Her fans love her for being successful in the mainstream without hiding her Latino roots.

Furthermore, Jennifer has succeeded where many other artists have failed miserably. Many stars, having become successful in one area, try to cross over into another: a dancer tries to become a singer; a singer tries to become an actor; an actor tries to make it in the dance world—most of these attempts end in failure. But Jennifer Lopez has rocketed to success in all these areas, becoming a dancer for Janet Jackson, a Golden Globe–nominated actress, and a platinum-selling singer. Perhaps no other artist in the world has managed the same explosive crossover success as Jennifer has had.

Today Jennifer Lopez is one of the music industry's biggest stars. She is one of the highest-paid actresses in Hollywood, reportedly making $15 million for just one of her movie roles. She has adoring fans all over the world, owns multi-million-dollar homes, and hangs with her fellow celebrities. But life was not always this way. There was a time when Jennifer trekked from disappointing audition to disappointing audition with her belongings in a backpack slung over her shoulder. Those were hard times, when she could only dream of getting that big break while she slept on a dance studio floor.

Though she was born and raised in New York, Jennifer Lopez's parents came to the country from Puerto Rico. Her heritage is very important to her. In this photo, Jennifer is shown on the MTV TR3's float at the 50th Annual Puerto Rican Day Parade.

The Girl From Castle Hill

Jennifer Lopez was born on July 24, 1969, in one of the toughest areas of New York City. She grew up in a neighborhood called Castle Hill, in a section of the city called the Bronx. It was a tough area, but it was also exciting and vibrant. In the 1970s, when Jennifer was a young girl, the Bronx was giving birth to a new culture called hip-hop. The music, dance, art, fashions, and language of that culture were exploding on the streets, and they would eventually change Jennifer and the world.

Jennifer explained to Prairie Miller of NY Rock that growing up in the Bronx shaped her as a person and as an artist. Today she's a big Hollywood star and tops the *Billboard* charts. She has wealth and fame, and she travels the world. But, as she said in the interview, you can take the girl out of the Bronx, but you can't take the Bronx out of the girl:

"For me, the Bronx is everything that I am. It manifests itself in everything that I do. Like it comes out in my songs and the different interviews that I do. And I think people think it's more of a calculated thing. And it's so funny, because things are so much more simple than everybody makes them out to be. . . . You know, it's really just that I grew up in the Bronx. I spent most of my first twenty years there. That's where all the foundation of the person that I am comes from. And that's not gonna go away. And I'm sorry if everybody doesn't wanna hear about it, but that's just the God's honest truth. And it's gonna come out constantly, because that's who I am. I'm a Puerto Rican girl from the Bronx."

Bronx-Born Girl

Jennifer's parents, Guadalupe and David, were both born in Puerto Rico and moved to New York City as young children. They later met, married, and had three daughters: Leslie, Jennifer, and Lynda. The girls' grandmother spoke only Spanish, but their parents spoke perfect English. Guadalupe and David wanted their daughters to speak English so they wouldn't face discrimination, so that became the language of their home. Nevertheless, the girls grew up with a mix of Puerto Rican and American *culture*.

Growing up Puerto Rican in the Bronx wasn't the easiest life. At that time, the Castle Hill neighborhood, along with the Bronx in general, underwent significant changes. Most were not for the better. The Bronx was in decline. For much of its history, the borough was a mix of people from all over the world, with Germans, Italians, Jews, Latin Americans, and

Jennifer grew up in Castle Hill, one of the toughest neighborhoods in the deteriorating Bronx. Still, her parents were able to shield her from much of the worst parts of the neighborhood.

African Americans living in its neighborhoods. But by the 1960s, the borough was deteriorating, and its residents were fleeing to other parts of the city, suburbs, and even to other states.

Many factors contributed to the Bronx's deterioration. One of the largest was an expressway that cut a scar across the city, separating and destroying the neighborhoods in its path. Another was an explosion of high-density housing projects for people with low incomes. But instead of bettering the resident's lives, the projects created concentrated areas of poverty and crime.

By the 1970s, the people with enough money to do so had fled the changing Bronx neighborhoods. The poorest residents, most of whom were African American or Latino, were left behind to face falling property values, declining schools, and increasing crime. Arsons plagued the borough, especially on the south side, and gave birth to the famous phrase, "The Bronx is burning." It was a harsh world marred by poverty, crime, and hopelessness, and Castle Hill became one of the toughest neighborhoods in this harsh world.

Jennifer's Bronx neighborhood might have been one of the most dangerous around, but as she explained in an interview with *Reader's Digest*, that was not the life she knew. She said she didn't learn about the crime and struggles that went on in her neighborhood until she was much older. Jennifer explained that it may have been the tough inner city, but it was also home:

"I only found out when I was in my 20s and dated a cop who worked in my neighborhood. I told him I grew up on Castle Hill, and he said, 'That's the worst crime area.' I knew nothing of it. My parents had three girls and raised us to do the right things—go to school, get good grades, try to get into college. It was about trying to have a better life. We weren't allowed to hang out on the streets. Parties—God forbid. I'd beg

for weeks to go, then have to be home by 11 p.m., when everybody else was just getting there."

Influenced by the Street

Jennifer's attentive parents shielded her from the street. The girls enjoyed music and dancing, and their mother encouraged them to put on living-room productions for the family's entertainment. Jennifer began taking dance classes at her local Boys & Girls Club when she was five. She attended Catholic school, and although she wasn't a top student, she was a gifted athlete. Her favorite movie was *West Side Story*, a Romeo-and-Juliet story of a Puerto Rican girl and Polish-American boy who fall in love but are torn apart by violence between the American and Puerto Rican gangs. It was a story Jennifer could relate to, one that expressed both the dreams and the heartaches people experienced in neighborhoods like hers.

Jennifer's parents tried to provide wholesome entertainment at home and protect her and her sisters from the realities just beyond their door, but the street's rhythms still reached her ears and got into her soul. While the Bronx was crumbling under urban decay, its people were searching for hope amid the misery that engulfed their neighborhoods. The struggle to find pleasure, meaning, and purpose in a depressing, dangerous, and uncertain corner of New York City gave birth to a new form of art and culture.

Throughout human history, people have turned to art for enjoyment, communication, and inspiration. People can express their deepest thoughts and most complex emotions through art. They can tell people the story of their lives through a poem, a paintbrush, a dance, or a song. Creating, enjoying, and participating in art can lift people from their circumstances and make them part of something better, something greater, something special.

Young people in the Bronx in the 1970s didn't have much to look forward to. They didn't have a lot to make them feel

Music has always been important to Jennifer and her sisters. It was also important to others living in the Bronx, the birthplace of hip-hop. It was a way to tell stories about the way life really was.

great or special. But they started making new forms of art, and their efforts became a cultural revolution that would one day affect music, fashion, language, and cultures all over the world.

The Birth of Hip-Hop

The parties that Jennifer's parents carefully kept her from were the heart of this new cultural and artistic movement. People in the Bronx may not have had much, but they could have fun, and music and dancing were the entertainment of choice. DJs set up sound systems, spinning funk, soul, and disco records, and throngs of people gathered in clubs, the streets, and parks to party. If there wasn't an electrical outlet for the DJ's equipment, it was no problem: they simply hotwired streetlights for their power. Running on stolen juice, they cranked up the music, and people danced away their troubles.

The best DJs were the ones with the best dance music. When DJs—one named Kool Herc in particular—introduced a Jamaican style of *cutting* and *mixing* to make their music more danceable, hip-hop was born. The most danceable part of a song is the part that contains just the beat, also called the break. The problem for a dance party, however, is that the break is usually short. Kool Herc realized that, using two turntables, each with a record, and a mixer, he could isolate the break, mix back and forth between the two records, and keep the beat going as long as he desired. That allowed partiers to dance on and on. It was a revolutionary innovation, and other Bronx and New York City DJs jumped onboard. They elevated turntables to instruments and made spinning records an art form.

Kool Herc didn't just work the turntables. He also worked the microphone. As the music pumped, he'd emcee (or MC), entertaining the crowd with jokes, stories, banter, boasts, or anything that came to mind. Soon MCs began speaking to the music in complex rhythms and rhymes. The style became known as rapping, and it became an art form of its own.

While DJs were mixing and MCs rapping, tagging (or graffiti) developed as the visual expression of hip-hop culture. Many people think graffiti is just a form of vandalism, but others realize graffiti is part of a whole **underground** movement of expression and rebellion that has become an art. In the beginning, tagging was just a name or number scrawled on a subway car or city bus, a way to say "I was here." But the graffiti grew colorful, complex, and thought provoking, becoming an important element of street culture.

If DJing and MCing were hip-hop's musical expression, and graffiti was its visual expression, then b-boying (also called break dancing) was its physical expression. Break dancing is a highly improvisational, rhythmic, and acrobatic dance form. Break-dancers combined complex footwork with full-body moves, gymnastics, and even martial arts techniques to create a new type of dance that required incredible skill, strength, and power. B-boying became one more element of the hip-hop movement, and it inspired the hip-hop dance style that is popular today.

Hip-Hop Makes Its Mark

The energy and excitement of hip-hop was contagious, and the 1979 single "Rapper's Delight" by the Sugarhill Gang was the first mainstream success of a hip-hop song. It hit #36 on the U.S. pop charts and #3 on the UK singles chart. "I was in third grade when 'Rapper's Delight' changed my life," Jennifer said in an interview.

The impact of "Rapper's Delight" on ten-year-old Jennifer was life-altering, but she remained nurtured by other sounds as well, like Motown—a soulful musical style that originated in Detroit—and the music of her Latin American roots. She remembers listening to hip-hop on the streets, then coming home to other music. "My mother would be listening to Celia

Cruz, Tito Puente, Diana Ross. I want to include all those elements in my music."

Her mother's musical tastes were one lasting and important influence of growing up in the Lopez home. But other elements of growing up under her parents' guidance contributed to her success later in life. In an interview with Todd Gilchrist for blackfilm.com, Jennifer talked about her upbringing and how it made her confident, hardworking, and driven to succeed:

> *"I think my mom was very integral in that part of my life because she just kind of made us believe that we could do anything. She always was very big on us being independent, not having to depend on any man, not having to depend on anybody, just being able to kind of survive on your own no matter what. And one of the things that went along with that was working hard—always working hard. And they were great examples. My dad worked nights most of my life. My mom worked at the school and had a Tupperware job; that was how our upbringing was, so work was always a very big part of my life and also, she really made us believe that we could do anything. You know, we could be the President of the United States if we wanted to, if we worked hard enough—a Puerto Rican girl from New York—and it seems so far-fetched, but when people make you believe that, you do."*

There was one thing, however, that Jennifer's mother did not encourage her to do: become a professional dancer. Jennifer had been dancing since she was five years old, and her parents had always encouraged the activity. But when Jennifer decided she was going to give up on higher education to pursue dancing, her mother told her she'd have to do it on her own.

The United States has long been known as the land of opportunity, and Jennifer Lopez has taken full advantage of the doors that have opened for her. She worked hard and was very talented, but she also had to take her share of rejection along the way.

Out on Her Own

Jennifer's grandparents and parents had come to America because they believed it was the land of opportunity; it was a place where people could build a better life. They believed the best way to build that life was to do well in school, get a college education, and have a respectable, well-paying career as a lawyer or a businessperson. Becoming a professional dancer didn't sound like a path to a better life at all. It sounded like a road to rejection, poverty, and heartache.

Jennifer was sixteen when she got her first taste of serious acting by landing a small role in the film *My Little Girl*. The experience was intoxicating and made her more determined than ever to become a performer. Nevertheless, when she graduated from high school, she followed her parents' wishes and enrolled in Baruch College. Her parents had always taught her to work hard, and she worked at a law office while going to school. But dancing was still her passion, and though she studied and worked by day, she took dance classes by night.

The crazy schedule was too much. Jennifer couldn't juggle it all, and by the end of her first semester at school she knew she had to give up something. She couldn't bear to give up her dreams, so she dropped out of school instead. From now on, she was going to put all her energy into building a dance career. Her parents were not impressed.

The Lean Years

Jennifer's parents were angry and scared. They had worked so hard to give their girls a bright future. Now Jennifer was going to risk it all on a dream of being a *performer*. They made it clear that if she was going to drop out of school and pursue show business, she was going to have to do it on her own. She packed her belongings and moved out of her parents' home. She had won a scholarship to study dance, and now she found herself sleeping at times on the dance studio floor. She had nowhere else to go, and for a long time she had no promising dancing jobs either.

Jennifer got a music video here, a club performance there, but nothing that could regularly pay the bills, let alone make her a star. The first hint of something bigger came in 1991 when, after many unsuccessful auditions, she was invited to take a guest spot at the American Music Awards as a backup dancer for a New Kids on the Block performance. But there were still many more rejections than victories, and the victories she did have were small. As the rejections and pressure mounted, Jennifer began to feel the strain.

After her appearance at the American Music Awards, Jennifer auditioned to be a Fly Girl—a member of the dance company—on one of America's hottest new shows, *In Living*

Color, a sketch-comedy show with a decidedly urban, hip-hop style. Failing the audition was a bitter blow. Perhaps Jennifer wouldn't make it as a dancer. Perhaps all her dreams really would go up in smoke, and her parents would be proved right after all.

The First Big Break

Shortly after her big *In Living Color* disappointment, Jennifer got a break she desperately needed. She landed a spot in a dance show called *Synchronicity*, which would tour Japan. As far as show-biz breaks go, it wasn't a huge one, but Jennifer was thrilled. She'd be able to dance and see a different part of the world. The experience, however, wasn't all positive. She began to realize how physically and emotionally demanding it is to be a touring dancer with constant rehearsals followed by performances. Even harder was the homesickness that plagued her.

When Jennifer returned from Japan, her big break was waiting at her door. Back in Hollywood, some minds had changed. They wanted her on *In Living Color* after all. She moved to California and began her life as a Fly Girl. Her homesickness in Hollywood was perhaps even worse than it had been in Japan, and Jennifer wasn't entirely happy with her new job. But she also now knew that homesickness and sacrifice came with the territory. It was a lesson that she had her mom to thank for.

When she telephoned her mother to vent about her frustrations and sadness, she expected to find a sympathetic ear and some comfort. Instead, her mother told her to toughen up. Show business was hard, her mother said, and if Jennifer wanted to succeed, she had better learn to accept the sacrifices. It might not been what she wanted to hear, but it was exactly what Jennifer needed to hear. After the conversation, she redoubled her efforts. This was the life she had chosen, and it was the one she wanted. She took that attitude into her

Jennifer got her big break as a dancer on the television show *In Living Color*. As a Fly Girl on the show, her career was ready to explode. Soon she was a regular at award shows. In this photo, Jennifer is seen arriving for Nickelodeon's 17th Annual Kids' Choice Awards.

work on *In Living Color* and eventually became the lead Fly Girl.

Taking the Plunge

In Living Color would make a number of people famous. Jim Carrey, Jamie Foxx, and Chris Rock, not to mention the show's creators the Wayans brothers, all used the show as a springboard to launch huge careers. The show would be a springboard for Jennifer as well. After two seasons, she gave up being a Fly Girl. She landed a part as a backup dancer in Janet Jackson's music video for "That's the Way Love Goes" and was offered a chance to accompany Janet on her world tour. It was a huge opportunity that most dancers would jump at. But Jennifer had other things in mind. She was ready to start her acting career.

She was dreaming of the big screen, but Jennifer's first acting jobs had her on the television screen instead. She played nurse Rosie Romero in the made-for-television movie, *The Crash of Flight 7*. Then she had roles in three short-lived television series: *Second Chances, South Central,* and *Hotel Malibu*. Jennifer performed well. Unfortunately, none of the shows lasted long. That, however, would turn out to be a blessing in disguise as movie roles were just around the corner.

The first major screen role to come Jennifer's way was in the film *My Family*. It was the story of three generations of a Mexican American family in California. Jennifer played an American citizen who is illegally deported to Mexico and must find her way back across the border. Jennifer didn't have the largest role in the film, but she did have a heart-pounding, show-stealing scene in which she battles across dangerous river waters while carrying a baby in her arms.

Jennifer's performance in *My Family* got people's attention and began a string of roles that would see Jennifer appearing alongside some of Hollywood's biggest stars. She joined Wesley Snipes and Woody Harrelson in the action blockbuster *Money*

Train, starred with Robin Williams in *Jack*, and worked with Jack Nicholson and Judy Davis in *Blood and Wine*.

The Role of Her Life

Jennifer had worked through lean years, disappointing rejections, and self-doubt; now, finally, her career was on a roll. And things were just about to get better. Rumor had it that a film was in the works about the life and death of a woman named Selena Quintanilla.

Selena was a Mexican American singer who released her first album at the age of twelve and was an icon by the time she turned twenty. She was the **Tejano** music world's brightest star. In 1994, she won a Grammy Award, and it looked like she was about to break out into the mainstream; she was planning the release of her first English album for 1995. That album, however, would never be finished. Before the album's completion, Selena was shot by her fan-club president, Yolanda Saldívar. She died in the hospital a few hours later. Selena was twenty-three years old. Her fans were devastated, and tens of thousands of people attended her funeral.

A few months after her death, Selena became the mainstream success she had hoped to be in life. Her record label released *Dreaming of You*, a mixture of her Spanish songs and some of the English-language songs she had recorded before her death. The album debuted at #1 on the *Billboard* 200 album chart and went on to sell approximately five million copies in the United States alone.

In 1997, the film *Selena* hit the big screen, telling the story of the singer's amazing life and tragic death. Thousands of people auditioned to play the part of Selena, but Jennifer Lopez landed the role. It was the biggest success of her career so far, and she was nominated for the Golden Globe award for Best Actress in a Musical. The film was big for Jennifer for another reason. Filming concert scenes, standing onstage before a stadium of Selena's fans, convinced Jennifer that she too wanted to be a singer.

A New Life

Her role in *Selena* marked a whole new stage in Jennifer's career and personal life. On the career front, she was now a star, and a well-paid one at that. She was reportedly paid one million dollars for her role in the film, becoming the first

Selena was the first female to achieve success in male-dominated Tejano music. When Jennifer played her in the film *Selena*, it was a wake-up call for the young performer. Jennifer knew that she, too, wanted to be a singer.

Latina actress to cross the million-dollar mark for a movie. More movies followed, and she began working to launch a music career.

On the personal front, 1997 was a big year for Jennifer as well. That's when she married her first husband, Ojani Noa. Jennifer met Ojani while still working on *Blood and Wine* with Jack Nicholson. The relationship shot into high gear right out of the gate, and shortly after filming was through on *Selena*, they got engaged. In February 1997, they got married. The time it took the relationship to develop, however, is about how long it took for the marriage to sour. Just a little over a year later, Jennifer and Ojani divorced, and Jennifer would be learning some hard lessons on how star's personal lives become media fodder.

Around this time, the media became enthralled with Jennifer for another reason: her body. After Selena, a number of big roles followed, the biggest being her part in the hit movie *Out of Sight* with George Clooney. It was Jennifer's most successful film to date, and suddenly everyone was in love with her . . . and her curves. Most of the talk centered on Jennifer's behind, which by Hollywood standards was downright big. At five feet, six inches and curvaceous, Jennifer showed women didn't have to be tall and stick-thin to be sexy.

Many actresses, after landing in Hollywood and finding their figures are topics of discussion, rush to lose weight. Not Jennifer. She had always been proud of her body, and she took a decidedly, "If you've got it, flaunt it!" approach. Soon she was as famous for her sexy style and revealing clothes as for her movie roles.

More to Buzz About

In 1999, Jennifer launched a new high-profile relationship and a new career, and she gave the entertainment industry a whole lot more to talk about. To help launch her music career, Jennifer collaborated with some big-name artists. She did a duet with Latin music sensation Marc Anthony, and she was featured in a music video for Sean "Puffy" Combs, who at the time went by the stage name Puff Daddy.

Shortly after appearing in Puff Daddy's video, Jennifer appeared on Puff Daddy's arm. The tabloids were suddenly ablaze with headlines about Hollywood's newest couple. Jennifer's relationship with Sean Combs, however, wasn't just romantic. It was business as well. He was one of the producers on the album she was about to release.

On June 1, 1999, On the 6, Jennifer's first album, debuted and climbed up the *Billboard* 200 album list, making it all the way to #8. The album's first single, "If You Had My Love," also became Jennifer's first #1 hit as it climbed to the top spot of the *Billboard* Hot 100 chart. Other singles, including "Waiting for Tonight" and "Let's Get Loud," also became big hits. The album drew a Grammy nomination for "Best Dance Recording" for the single "Let's Get Loud."

The album's title, *On the 6*, referred to the number 6 subway line Jennifer used to ride in her early years in Castle Hill. But she was a long way from the Bronx and its subway lines now. *On the 6* went triple platinum, selling more than three million copies in the United States and millions more worldwide. The album also confirmed that Jennifer was now a triple threat: a dancer, an actress, and a music star.

Jennifer Lopez always provides glitz and glam to any red-carpet event. In this photo, she and then-boyfriend Ben Affleck attend the premiere of their film *Gigli*. The film bombed, and eventually so did their relationship.

Jenny From the Block

Jennifer Lopez was everywhere. She was a movie star with a number of successful films under her belt. She was widely praised as one of the sexiest women alive. *People* magazine named her one of its "50 Most Beautiful People." Now she had a **platinum**-selling album. There could be no doubt, 1999 was an amazing year for her career. Unfortunately, the year that started with a bang was about to end with a scandal.

Scandal and Bad Press

Hollywood's good girl and rap's bad boy were an item, and in December 1999, that item ran into big trouble. Jennifer and Sean were at a nightclub in New York City when Sean and some members of his group got into a confrontation with other club goers. Things got heated, and gunshots rang out. In the chaos that followed, people raced from the nightclub and to their waiting cars.

The police stopped and searched the car carrying Sean and Jennifer, turning up a stolen gun. They hauled Jennifer and Sean downtown.

Jennifer was soon released, and when it was determined that she had no direct involvement with the shooting or the stolen gun, no charges were filed against her. Sean's legal mess went on much longer, but eventually he was acquitted of all charges. Jennifer and Sean kept their rocky relationship going through the legal battle, but officially announced their split shortly after Sean's trial ended.

During this period, Jennifer had other problems with the media as well. Not only were people sniffing around every aspect of her personal life, but Jennifer (now called J. Lo by her many fans) had built a reputation as a difficult **diva**. She caught flack for criticizing other famous actresses, and she sometimes came across as irritable in interviews. She was now deep in a relationship with Cris Judd, one of her former backup dancers. Within months of splitting with Sean, Jennifer married Cris. But this second marriage was even shorter than her first, ending in divorce less than a year later.

The tabloids couldn't get enough of J. Lo, painting her as a diva who couldn't be pleased and who changed men like she changed her shoes. In 2001, Jennifer told Prairie Miller of *NY Rock* that the press had her all wrong. Rather than a high-strung snob with an impulsive attitude toward men, Jen described herself as a hopeless romantic and a total goofball:

> *"I love all things romantic. . . . I'm very open with my love. I'm passionate and I feel a lot, and I'm never afraid to get close to someone. I'm not afraid of love. . . . But I can be the silliest and goofiest as they come. I grew up in the Bronx where you would stay up late with your girlfriends, just being silly in our bedrooms, whatever. And I was always the clown."*

Still a Career Girl

Jennifer tried not to let the media madness interfere with her career. In 2000, while the Puff Daddy gun controversy loomed like a dark cloud, Jennifer's psychological thriller, *The Cell*, created a buzz with its disturbing storyline and stunning visuals. In 2001, as her breakup and marriage grabbed tabloid headlines, her career made more impressive headlines when her new movie, *The Wedding Planner*, and new album, *J. Lo*, debuted at #1 in the same week. With a #1 movie at the box office and a #1 album on the charts, no one could deny that the most noteworthy thing about Jennifer Lopez was still her amazing talent and career.

By the time Jennifer released her second album, she felt that she was maturing in the show-biz world. She was starting to understand what it meant to live in the public eye, and she worked on improving her relationship with the media. She also worked on becoming a better artist. Her second album featured more of her own songs and attempted to be personal as well as entertaining. In her *NY Rock* interview, she said *J. Lo* was a very personal album:

> "The songs on J. Lo are more personal than before. The songs reflect a lot of what I've witnessed my sisters and my girlfriends going through. They're about relationships, and about having a good time and not having such a good time, or partying a lot and partying too much. It's all very much my point of view. . . . [It's] also an **homage** to my fans. [J. Lo is] what fans call me on the streets, and I like it. So giving the album this title is my way of telling them that this is for them, in appreciation of their support."

J. Lo sold millions of copies, eventually being certified quadruple platinum. In 2002, Jennifer gave another shout-out to

Once she made the decision to become a singer, Jennifer poured her heart into performing. In 2001, she had a #1 movie and an album debut at #1 at the same time, something no one had done before.

her fans with the release of her third album, this one a remix album called *J to the L-O!: The Remixes*. The album featured guest artists Fat Joe, Nas, and P. Diddy and was the most hip-hop album of her music career. It debuted in the #1 spot on the *Billboard* 200 chart, the first remix album to accomplish such a feat, and became her third platinum-selling album in a row. Later that year, she released her fourth album, *This Is Me . . . Then*. That album climbed to #3 on the charts, while the single "All I Have" became a #1 *Billboard* Hot 100 hit. The single "Jenny from the Block" did almost as well, peaking at #3. The album would be another multi-platinum hit for the acting, singing superstar.

Jenny from the Block

Workaholic Jennifer Lopez couldn't let 2002 go by without some movie work as well. Her biggest film of that year was *Maid in Manhattan*. Making the film was a type of homecoming for "Jenny from the Block." It was filmed in the Bronx, where she grew up, and the storyline was one she could relate to. The main character, Marisa Ventura, is a maid working in a Manhattan hotel, struggling as a single mom and hoping for a better life for her family. One day, Marisa gives in to temptation and tries on an expensive outfit belonging to a wealthy guest. On that same fateful day, a candidate for the U.S. Senate is staying in the hotel. He spots Marisa, is instantly intrigued by the beautiful woman, and wants to see her again.

When the would-be senator sees Marisa in her maid's clothing, he doesn't even notice her, let alone recognize her as the beautiful woman he flirted with just a short time before. Marisa dons beautiful clothing again, and the two find themselves quickly falling in love before Marisa's true identity is revealed and everything falls apart. Packaged in the framework of a simple romantic comedy, the story manages to touch on some complex tensions between personal relationships, social status, class, and ethnicity. Marisa, a Latina maid working for America's wealthy (and mostly white) elite, is a stereotype. But she's a stereotype purposely used to talk about some of the real inequalities that continue to affect American society.

In a 2002 interview, Jennifer told *NY Rock*'s Prairie Miller that working on the film brought her back to her roots and made her realize she hadn't changed that much:

> *"It really did bring back a lot of memories—filming up in the Bronx and everything. It just made me realize how far away from that character I'm not. It felt like the same exact thing, like I had never left the Bronx. It was such a good feeling. I was familiar with my surroundings. It was just easy, as far as the background of the character and all that. . . . You know, being from the Bronx and being Puerto Rican. I even told them on the set exactly how that man would look at her. It's just a weird kind of thing. It's a class thing. It's a social thing. It exists. To say that it doesn't exist would be a lie. It would be like trying to sugar coat the truth . . . you want people to respect you. Or look at you in the same way they look at everybody else. So that was definitely an emotion in the movie that I understand completely."*

There are critics, however, who feel that Jennifer's role in *Maid in Manhattan* is still a far cry from her *Selena* days. Despite the trailblazing success Jennifer has had with her career, there are those who think she has tried to soften her Latina image to make herself more mainstream. These critics argue that, like many Latina actresses in the past, Jennifer changed as her fame increased. For example, as the authors of *New Faces in a Changing America: Multiracial Identity in the 21st Century* write,

"This has been a disturbing aspect of the career of the Puerto-Rican American Jennifer Lopez. . . . In just 2 years, Lopez morphed from a dark-haired ethnic beauty wearing deep-toned cosmetics . . . to a blonde-streaked 'Diva Loca' . . . sporting make-up in pastel shades."

Jennifer, however, would definitely deny such accusations, saying her makeup and styles might change, but she'll always be "Jenny from the Block."

Jennifer has had to deal with the media prying into all parts of her life, especially her relationships. Many believe that the intense media attention caused Jennifer and Ben Affleck to break their engagement.

In another *NY Rock* interview, Jennifer talked about how facing everyone's judgment is a strain. She admitted that she sometimes feels misunderstood, but she tries to just keep moving forward and to let her work speak for itself:

"Absolutely, yeah, I do [feel misunderstood]. But you know, there's no way I can control that. I can only speak for myself, and hope people hear my words and see me on television speaking for myself. And, hopefully, they'll be able to make their own judgment. And at the end of the day, I just want my work to speak for itself. . . . I can control the music I make; I can control how I sing; how I dance; how I act in a movie, or how much time I put into this or that or the other. Like what I want to develop in the future. That's the only stuff I have control over. . . . If you think you can start controlling what image they put out there of you, you'll go nuts. A lot of times it's negative. They don't like to focus on the positive, no matter how much you do. You just have to put up like a defense mechanism as an artist, to not let the outside world come in and ruin that for you."

Back in the 'Bloids

As if hit albums and movies weren't enough, Jennifer also had the biggest Hollywood love story of 2002 and 2003. She and actor Ben Affleck got engaged, and their relationship generated a constant media circus. The tabloids dubbed the pair "Bennifer" and hounded them constantly. The wedding date was set for September 2003, but days before the ceremony, the media was filled with stories of trouble in paradise. The day came and went without any wedding bells, and a few months later, Bennifer was no more.

Jennifer and Ben went their separate ways, and soon married other people. Less than six months after their official breakup, Jennifer married Latin singing sensation Marc Anthony in a highly secret ceremony. Friends and family were reportedly invited to Jennifer's home for a party. It wasn't until they arrived that they realized they were there for a wedding.

On her third marriage and fifth serious relationship in seven years, there could be no avoiding comments in the media about Jennifer's tumultuous love life. Her marriage to Marc Anthony became a frequent focus of media speculation, everyone placing bets on how long it was going to last—a situation that hurt Jennifer, but that she tried not to focus on.

Unfortunately for Jennifer, in the years immediately after her marriage to Marc Anthony, she's had very little to pull the media's focus away from her love life. Her career continued, but none of her projects had headline-grabbing success. Her 2003 and 2004 movies, *Gigli* and *Jersey Girl*, were total flops. Things picked up with her next three movies: 2004's *Shall We Dance?* and 2005's *Monster-in-Law* and *An Unfinished Life*. Her music career, however, didn't follow suit. Her 2005 album, *Rebirth*, barely made a blip on the music world's radar screen. It debuted well at #2 on the *Billboard* 200 chart, but then fell off the charts, becoming her first album not to receive a platinum certification.

Jennifer Lopez turned her attention to other projects in 2006, but music was never too far from her mind. She has multi-tasking down to a fine art.

Finding Herself Again

In 2006, the world heard little from Jennifer Lopez. Her other business ventures, like her perfumes, clothing lines, body products, restaurant, and new production company marched on. But there was no movie. There was no album. Just as *Rebirth* had dropped off the charts, Jennifer Lopez dropped out of sight.

Jennifer's retreat from the media's prying eyes was probably to be expected. Over the years, tabloids had their field days with her over and over again, and she found ways to cope with the pressure. In one of her interviews with *NY Rock*, Jennifer admitted that it's hard to live with tabloid covers splashed with your name and people who track your every move. You lose your privacy and are always being examined and judged. She said that, for her, the best way to deal with the pressure is to just not pay attention:

"You have to develop a way to deal with it. And my way of dealing with it is to not even know what's going on. I don't know half the things they say, half the things they write, or half the rumors that are out there. I don't care. I don't care to know, and I don't ask anybody what's going on."

Keeping Sight of What's Important

After marrying Marc Anthony, Jennifer became much more private about her personal life and less open in interviews and with the media, trying to protect this marriage from the media spectacle that her other relationships endured. Jennifer has also always wanted to have children and a family. She has said that her marriage to Marc is the real deal, and speculation abounds that at least part of the reason for her withdrawal from the public eye is because she wants to focus on starting the family she's desired for so long.

Jennifer has used this time to reshape her career. Today, Jennifer is extremely thoughtful and introspective about her work. Many people go into the entertainment industry looking for fame and fortune. They don't necessarily think of film, music, and dance as art forms. They see them as a way to achieve celebrity status. Jennifer, however, says she is an artist first, a celebrity second. In an interview with Wilson Morales for blackfilm.com, Jennifer said her biggest challenge today is

One of J. Lo's new projects included marriage to fellow musician Marc Anthony. They had known each other for many years, and even dated earlier in their careers. Fans and family hope that Jennifer has finally found the person with whom she'll be happy.

In 2007, Jennifer released her first Spanish-language album. To Jennifer, this was an important album, another way for her to pay respect to her heritage.

making sure the media frenzy surrounding her personal life doesn't pollute her art:

> *"I think the biggest challenge I've faced over the past few years is keeping the image away from the artist. You know what I mean? Separating the work from the actual person. I used to think it was so much more sexy back in the day when it wasn't so much about people's personal lives as it was about the work that they do. It was controlled—I hate to say that in front of the press—but it was more controlled by the studio system. There was a mystery to our stars back then. That's why we can look at them still. Yeah, we find things out about them eventually—Elvis Presley was really this—but it's OK because we had the illusion for a while. When you watch their movies there is so much more impact because you didn't know who they were dating or if they were married or if they were walking around barefoot acting stupid. It doesn't matter to the work, but it does now. And that's been the biggest challenge for me."*

Jennifer certainly hasn't disappeared completely. At the end of the day, Jennifer just wants her home life to be private and her public life to be about her work and artistry.

True to Herself

Jennifer admits that the experience of fame has changed her. She told Morales that she has learned she needs to protect herself in an industry that will chew people up and spit them out for a juicy story:

> *"I'm just trying to get the focus back on what I do, what I do as an artist and not what I do when I'm at*

home. I've always had this kind of attitude—maybe it's the Bronx in me or whatever—where I've always been out there. I'm very open. I'm a free spirit by nature so I didn't think about what I was doing. But this business has changed me. I didn't want it to, but it changed me. It made me a much more reclusive, private person. As you get older—and I've been in the business over 15 years now—and as you experience and go through different things you realize you have to set boundaries. You have to for your life. You have to say this is OK and this is not OK. This is what I do for a living and this is my life. It's the only one I get and so I have to set boundaries. That's the approach I'm trying to take now, to get the focus back on what I do. I'm a singer. I'm an actress. I'm a dancer. That's what I do."

In 2007, the public got a look at how Jennifer had spent part of 2006, when two major films were released. She was now concentrating on projects that had meaning for her rather than on what was most likely to be a mainstream success. The first film was *Bordertown*, a movie based on the true story of an American journalist who goes to Ciudad Juárez, a town on the Mexican side of the Mexico-U.S. border, to investigate the murders of numerous women.

Jennifer was honored with the Artists for Amnesty International award for helping to shed light on the continuing murders in this border city. Jennifer followed *Bordertown* with *El Cantante*, another real-life tale, this one based on **salsa** singer Hector Lavoe. Marc Anthony plays Hector in the film. Both movies show a rebirth of Jennifer as a serious actress.

Marc also worked closely with Jennifer on her newest album. In March 2007, Jennifer released her first Spanish-language album, *Como Ama una Mujer*, which in English means

How a Woman Loves. The album has done well, making the top 10 of the *Billboard* 200 chart. Overall, Jennifer's work in 2007 sends the message that she wants to get back to making serious art that is meaningful to her and reflects her heritage. So far, it seems her fans are ready to go along for the ride.

July 24,
1969   Jennifer Lopez is born in New York City.

1970s   Hip-hop is born in the Bronx.

1979   The Sugarhill Gang's "Rapper's Delight" becomes the first hip-hop song to achieve mainstream success.

1986   Jennifer lands her first movie role.

1990–
1992   Jennifer appears as a Fly Girl on the television show *In Living Color*.

1991   Jennifer performs as a backup dancer at the American Music Awards.

1995   Jennifer gets her first major film role in *My Family*.

1997   Jennifer plays the title role in the film *Selena*, and receives a Golden Globe nomination for her performance.

Jennifer marries Ojani Noa.

1999   Sean "Puffy" Combs and Jennifer begin a relationship.

People names her one of its "50 Most Beautiful People."

June 1,
1999   *On the 6*, Jennifer's first album, is released.

**Dec.
1999** Jennifer and Sean Combs are questioned regarding a shooting at a nightclub.

2001 Jennifer marries Cris Judd; they divorce a few months later.

She has the #1 album and the #1 film debut in the same week.

2002 Jennifer and Ben Affleck begin a relationship.

2003 "Bennifer" break up after their wedding date comes and goes without a ceremony.

**June 5,
2004** Jennifer marries Marc Anthony, one week after his divorce is finalized.

2006 Jennifer and Marc star in *El Cantante*.

2007 Jennifer mentors contestants and performs on *American Idol*.

Her work on the film *Bordertown*, bringing the murders of women in Mexico to the public's attention, earns her an award from Amnesty International.

**March
2007** Her first Spanish-language album is released.

Albums

1999   *On the 6*

2001   *J.Lo*

2002   *J to tha L-O! The Remixes*

2002   *This Is Me . . . Then*

2005   *Rebirth*

2007   *Como Ama una Mujer*

Number-One Singles

1999   "If You Had My Love"

2000   "Feelin' so Good" (with Big Pun and Fat Joe)

2001   "I'm Real"

2001   "I'm Real" (Murder Remix with Ja Rule and Nas)

2003   "All I Have" (with LL Cool J)

2004   "Get Right"

2007   "Qué Hiciste"

Films

1986   *My Little Girl*

1995   *My Family*

1995	*Money Train*
1996	*Jack*
1996	*Blood and Wine*
1997	*Selena*
1997	*Anaconda*
1997	*U-Turn*
1998	*Out of Sight*
1998	*Antz* (voice)
2000	*The Cell*
2001	*The Wedding Planner*
2001	*Angel Eyes*
2002	*Enough*
2002	*Maid in Manhattan*
2003	*Gigli*
2003	*Jersey Girl*
2004	*Shall We Dance?*
2005	*Monster-in-Law*
2005	*An Unfinished Life*
2006	*Bordertown*
2006	*El Cantante*

DVDs

2000 *Feelin' so Good*

2003 *Let's Get Loud*

2003 *The Reel Me*

Awards and Recognition

1998 ALMA Award: Outstanding Actress (*Selena*).

1999 ALMA Award: Outstanding Actress (*Out of Sight*); Ritmo Latino Awards: Best New Artist of the Year; *Billboard* Music Award: Best Pop Clip ("If You Had My Love"); Teen Choice Award: Best Song of the Summer ("If You Had My Love"); VH1/Vogue Fashion Award: Most Fashionable Female Artist.

2000 MTV Video Music Award: Best Dance Video (*Waiting for Tonight*); MTV Movie Award: Best Dressed in a Movie (*The Cell*); MTV Europe Music Award: Best R&B; VH1/Vogue Fashion Award: the Versace Award; Nickelodeon Kids' Choice Award: Favorite New Music Artist; Bambi: Best International Pop Performance; ALMA Award: Outstanding Music Video Performer (*If You Had My Love*); *Billboard* Latin Music Award: Hot Latin Track of the Year, Vocal Duo ("No Me Ames" with Marc Anthony).

2001   Stinkers Bad Movie Awards: Most Annoying Fake Accent—Female (*Angel Eyes*); ALMA Awards: Outstanding Music Video—People's Choice Award (*Love Don't Cost a Thing*), Outstanding Actress—Motion Picture (*Angel Eyes*); MTV Europe Music Awards: Best Female; Nickelodeon Kids' Choice Award: Favorite Female Movie Star; Teen Choice Award: Best Dance Track ("Play").

2002   MTV Video Music Award: Best Hip-Hop Video (*I'm Real*); MTV Europe Music Award: Best Female; VH1/Vogue Fashion Award: Most Influential Artist; ShoWest Award: Female Star of the Year; Teen Choice Award: Best R&B/Hip-Hop/Rap Single ("Ain't It Funny—Murder Remix"); World Music Award: World's Best-Selling Latin Female Artist.

2003   American Music Award: Favorite Pop/Rock Female Artist; Golden Raspberry Awards: Worst Actress (*Gigli*), Worst Screen Couple (*Gigli*, with Ben Affleck); Teen Choice Awards: Female Fashion Icon, Best R&B/Hip-Hop Artist; NRJ Radio Award: Best R&B; *Billboard* Latin Music Award: Best-Selling Latin Dance Single of the Year ("Alive").

2004   *Billboard* Latin Music Award: Best-Selling Latin Dance Single of the Year ("I'm Glad").

2006 Women in Film: Crystal Award; Groovevolt Music & Fashion Award: Most Fashionable Music Video (*Get Right*); ACE Award for Accessories.

2007 *Us Weekly*: Style Icon of the Year; Amnesty International: Artists for Amnesty International Award.

Books

Baker, Trevor. *Jennifer Lopez*. London: Carlton Books, 2001.

Barnham, Kay. *Jennifer Lopez*. Chicago, Ill.: Raintree, 2005.

Chang, Jeff. *Can't Stop Won't Stop: A History of the Hip-Hop Generation*. New York: Picador, 2005.

Gallick, Sarah. *J.Lo: The Secret Behind Jennifer Lopez's Climb to the Top*. Boca Raton, Fla.: AMI Books, 2003.

Hill, Anne E. *Jennifer Lopez*. New York: Chelsea House, 2000.

Light, Alan (ed.). *The Vibe History of Hip Hop*. New York: Three Rivers Press, 1999.

Menard, Valerie. *Jennifer Lopez*. Hockessin, Del.: Mitchell Lane, 2003.

Parish, James Robert. *Jennifer Lopez: Actor and Singer*. New York: Ferguson Publishing Company, 2005.

Tracy, Kathleen. *Jennifer Lopez*. Toronto, Ont.: ECW Press, 2000.

Web Sites

Jennifer Lopez
www.biogs.com/famous/lopez.html

Jennifer Lopez on Biography
www.biography.com/search/article.do?id=9542231

Jennifer Lopez on MTV
www.mtv.com/music/artist/lopez_jennifer/artist.jhtml

Official Jennifer Lopez Site
www.jenniferlopez.com

culture—The beliefs, customs, practices, and social behavior of a particular nation or people.

cutting—Manually queuing up duplicate copies of the same record in order to repeatedly play the same passage.

diva—An extremely arrogant and glamorous woman, especially an actress or singer.

homage—A show of respect toward someone.

mainstream—The ideas, actions, and values that are most widely accepted by a group or society.

mentor—A more experienced person who provides advice and support to a less experienced person.

mixing—Blending sounds from different sources to come up with a new sound.

platinum—A designation indicating that a recording has sold at least 1 million copies.

R&B—Rhythm and blues; a style of music that combines blues and jazz and that was originally developed by African American musicians.

salsa—A type of Latin American dance music that combines elements of jazz and rock with African-Cuban melodies.

stereotypes—Oversimplified ideas about people, often based on incomplete and inaccurate information, held by one person or group about another person or group.

Tejano—Tex-Mex popular music combining elements of traditional, rock, and country music and often featuring an accordion.

underground—Separate from the main social or artistic environment.

Index

Affleck, Ben 34, 41, 42
American Idol 10
Amnesty International 50
Anthony, Marc 33, 43, 46, 50

Bordertown 50

The Cell 37
Combs, Sean 35–36
Como Ama una Mujer 50

DJ Kool Herc 21

El Cantante 50

Hip-Hop 21–23

J. Lo 37
Judd, Cris 36
J to the L-O!:The Remixes 39

Lopez, Jennifer
    acting career 10–12, 29–32, 37, 39–40, 43, 50
    body 32
    and the Bronx 5–21
    business ventures of, 45
    and college 26

and dance 23, 25–26, 29
and Latino Heritage of 10–12, 40–41
and *In Living Color* 26–29
marriage 32, 36, 43
and the media 32–33, 36–37, 42–46, 49
and romance 36
and singing 30–31, 33, 37–39, 50–51

Maid in Manhattan 39

Noa, Ojani 32

On the 6 33
Out of Sight 32

People Magazine 35

Rapper's Delight 22

Selena 30, 40
Selena Quintanilla 13, 30, 31

The Wedding Planner 37

Que Hiciste 9

About the Author

MaryJo Lemmens is a children's nonfiction writer who lives in Toronto, Ontario, Canada's largest city. Before moving to Toronto, she lived in the United States and South Africa. She received her bachelor's degree from Smith College in Northampton, Massachusetts. She has written numerous publications for young people.

Picture Credits